Mastering Real Estate Investment: Strategies for Success

I0436248

Logan M. Barnhouse

Written in 2022 and Finished and published in 2023
Revisions of 2022 text are updated for 2023 market cycle

2023 by Logan Barnhouse
ISBN: 9798857880470

Introduction: The Allure of Real Estate Investment

Real estate investment has long been hailed as a tried-and-true pathway to building wealth, achieving financial freedom, and securing a prosperous future. With its potential for steady cash flow, capital appreciation, and tax benefits, it's no wonder that many individuals are drawn to the world of real estate. However, navigating this complex landscape requires a solid understanding of market dynamics, financial strategies, and risk management.

In this book, "Mastering Real Estate Investment: Strategies for Success" we will embark on a journey through the fundamentals and intricacies of real estate investment. Whether you're a novice seeking to make your first investment or a seasoned investor looking to expand your portfolio, this comprehensive guide will equip you with the knowledge, tools, and insights needed to make informed decisions and succeed in the dynamic world of real estate.

Importance of Understanding the Real Estate Market

The real estate market is a dynamic ecosystem, influenced by a myriad of factors such as economic trends, population growth, interest rates, and consumer preferences. As an investor, it's crucial to recognize that success in real estate requires more than just luck; it demands a deep understanding of these market forces. By grasping the underlying dynamics that shape property values and investment opportunities, you'll be better positioned to identify lucrative ventures and navigate challenges with confidence.

Overview of the Book's Content

Throughout the chapters that follow, we will dive into the key facets of real estate investment, guiding you through the entire process from preparation to execution. We'll explore the different types of properties, delve into financing options, dissect investment strategies, and uncover effective ways to manage risk. Whether your goal is to generate passive income through rental properties, engage in property flipping for short-term gains, or build a diversified portfolio, this book will provide you with the tools and strategies to make informed decisions.

Remember, investing in real estate is not a one-size-fits-all endeavor. Each investor's journey is unique, influenced by personal financial goals, risk tolerance, and market conditions. By the time you reach the final chapter, you'll be armed with the insights and expertise to embark on your own successful real estate investment journey.

So, let's begin our exploration of the captivating world of real estate investment, starting with the foundational concepts that underpin this lucrative venture. Get ready to transform your financial future as we embark on a quest to master the art of real estate investment.

Chapter 1:
History of Real Estate Investment

Real estate investment is a dynamic and multifaceted endeavor that offers a tapestry of benefits and challenges for those willing to embark on this journey. Understanding these aspects is essential as you navigate the landscape of property ownership and seek to build a robust investment portfolio.

Benefits of Real Estate Investing:

Tax Advantages: Real estate investment grants you access to a realm of valuable tax advantages that can significantly impact your financial bottom line. Tax deductions on mortgage interest payments and property taxes can help reduce your taxable income, allowing you to retain a larger portion of your earnings. Furthermore, the concept of depreciation lets you deduct a portion of the property's value over time, lowering your tax liability even further. However, taxes can get very complicated. For example, there are potential ways to set up a 401(k) that can self fund through your rental properties but, rental income is specifically not allowed to fund a 401k. So, that requires having your rental business pay your management company that you own and then that management company make deposits into a 401(k). This is not something and inexperienced investor should explore without talking to tax consultants and getting advice from local trusted financial advisors.

Leverage for Growth: One of the most compelling aspects of real estate investing is the ability to leverage your money to magnify your returns. By using borrowed funds, you can control a larger asset while only investing a fraction of the total value. This leverage amplifies your potential gains, allowing you to grow your wealth more rapidly than traditional investment avenues. For example, if you purchase a $100,000 house and you have to put 20% to close, that comes to $20,000 out-of-pocket. What's that assume that your payment is $750 a month and your rent is $1000 a month. That's a profit of $250 a month you can then extrapolate that out for the year to be a total of $3000. If we also assume that a property would appreciate at 3% annually that's another $3000 of value added. Which means in one year we gain $3000 in cash flow $3000 in property appreciation total return on investment in one year $6000 and our cost was $20,000 where we then loaned the remainder of the purchase of $80,000 and that is someone else's money. In this scenario the ROI would be 30% in one year now it's worth noting that that is a very high percentage of return and it is based on the numbers that we used which is not a real property.

Appreciation and Equity Building: Real estate is a tangible asset that has historically demonstrated appreciation over time. As properties increase in value, your net worth naturally expands, and the equity you hold grows. Simultaneously, as you make mortgage payments, you're gradually paying down the loan principal, further enhancing your ownership stake.

Steady Cash Flow: Investing in rental properties can provide you with a reliable and consistent stream of cash flow. The rental income generated from tenants contributes to covering expenses, mortgage payments, and potentially even generating a surplus, which can be reinvested or used to support your lifestyle.

Stability and Inflation Hedge: Real estate investments are known for their relative stability, especially when compared to more volatile investment options. Properties tend to withstand economic fluctuations and provide a sense of security. Moreover, real estate acts as a hedge against inflation—property values and rental income have historically risen alongside the cost of living, helping preserve your purchasing power over time. Without getting too complicated it's worth understanding that typically real property value is tied to the amount of inflation happening within the US dollar. There are ways that you can improve your appreciation faster than the US dollar and due to lack of maintenance you can also slow your appreciation compared to the US dollar. Real estate is about preserving your buying power overtime while collecting cash flow.

Risks of Real Estate Investing:

Initial Capital Requirement: While real estate offers a pathway to wealth accumulation, it often demands a substantial initial capital investment. Acquiring properties requires funds for down payments, closing costs, and potential renovations, which can serve as a barrier to entry for some investors.

Long-Term Commitment: Real estate investment is not a get-rich-quick scheme; it requires patience and a long-term perspective. It may take years to realize significant returns on your investment, necessitating a commitment to withstand the test of time.

Property Management Challenges: Owning and managing properties entails responsibilities such as maintenance, repairs, tenant interactions, and adherence to local regulations. The complexities of property management can be time-consuming and financially demanding.

Market Volatility: Real estate markets can experience fluctuations, impacting property values and rental demand. Economic downturns may lead to decreased occupancy rates and rental income, affecting your investment returns.

Legal and Regulatory Considerations: Navigating the legal landscape of real estate investment involves an understanding of tenant rights, zoning laws, property taxes, and other regulations. Failure to comply with these requirements can result in financial and legal consequences.

In your pursuit of real estate investment success, it's crucial to weigh these benefits and risks carefully, conduct thorough research, and formulate a strategy that aligns with your financial goals and risk tolerance.

Understanding the differences between residential, commercial, and industrial properties is pivotal as you craft your investment strategy and determine the most suitable avenue to pursue.

Residential Properties:

Residential properties encompass single-family homes, duplexes, condominiums, apartment complexes, and other dwellings designed for personal habitation. These properties form the foundation of real estate investment for many individuals, presenting both advantages and considerations.

Larger Pool of Prospective Tenants: Residential properties cater to a broad demographic of individuals seeking a place to call home. This extensive tenant pool can help mitigate the risk of extended vacancies, ensuring a relatively steady stream of potential renters. It's not always valuable to have a large pool of tenants. Pricing your rental is important to find a balance between number of applications and quality of applications. I have found over the time that I have listed properties on social media for rent in rural America that you will get 10% of the total views will turn into messages, 1% of those will turn in the applications, and 1% of that 1% will be worth moving forward with.

Steady, Predictable Returns: While residential properties typically yield lower returns compared to commercial and industrial ventures, they offer a level of stability and predictability. Rental income from residential units contributes to regular cash flow, making them an attractive option for investors seeking consistent returns.

Easier Entry Point: Investing in residential properties often requires a lower initial capital investment, making it an accessible choice for those new to real estate. Additionally, property management for residential units may be less complex than for commercial or industrial properties.

Commercial Properties:

Commercial properties encompass office spaces, retail centers, hotels, and other establishments used for business purposes. Engaging in commercial real estate investment requires a deeper understanding of market dynamics and legal complexities.

Higher Potential Returns: Commercial properties have the potential to generate higher rental income and returns compared to residential properties. Long-term leases and businesses' willingness to pay a premium for prime locations contribute to increased profitability.

Long-Term Tenant Stability: Commercial leases often span multiple years, providing a level of tenant stability that may be absent in the residential sector. Businesses tend to establish roots and remain in their chosen locations, reducing the risk of frequent turnovers. However, with long tenants that may stay 10 years or more, these tenants put much effort and expenditure selecting the location, in turn meaning your vacancy between tenants could be a year or more all the while expenses still need to be paid.

Market Expertise Required: Investing in commercial properties demands a more comprehensive understanding of market trends, demand drivers, and tenant preferences. Effective management and successful leasing strategies necessitate an in-depth knowledge of the local commercial real estate landscape.

Industrial Properties:

Industrial properties encompass warehouses, distribution centers, manufacturing facilities, and other spaces designed for industrial activities. While often requiring a significant capital outlay, industrial properties offer distinct advantages.

High Returns and Long-Term Leases: Industrial properties can yield impressive returns, driven by the demand for specialized facilities. Long-term leases with established tenants contribute to a steady income stream, making industrial investments attractive for those seeking substantial profits. Industrial equipment is not easy of cheap to move, this could mean with good relationships you could have a lifelong tenant, however, markets change both positively and negatively. This mean that if a tenant leaves, just like a commercial property, you will need OPEX to continue paying the bills for the months to years between tenants.

Capital-Intensive Investments: Acquiring and maintaining industrial properties typically involves a higher capital investment compared to residential or even commercial properties. Robust infrastructure, specialized amenities, and compliance with industrial standards contribute to the initial costs.

Niche Market Expertise: Investing in industrial properties demands a unique set of skills and knowledge, including an understanding of logistical considerations, zoning regulations, and industry-specific requirements.

As you embark on your real estate investment journey, it's crucial to recognize the distinct characteristics of each property type and align your investment goals and risk tolerance accordingly. Whether you choose the stability of residential properties, the potentially higher returns of commercial ventures, or the niche opportunities presented by industrial properties, a comprehensive understanding of these differences will serve as your compass in navigating the diverse landscape of real estate investment.

In real estate investments, perhaps no single factor holds as much influence over the success of your endeavors as the strategic selection of location. The adage "location, location, location" resonates deeply within the real estate realm, and for good reason. The significance of location extends beyond mere proximity—it encompasses a complex interplay of demographic patterns, economic vibrancy, and future potential. Understanding how location intertwines with data-driven insights and market trends is essential for crafting a resilient and prosperous investment strategy.

The Significance of Location:

When considering a potential real estate investment, the location of the property can often determine its destiny. It's more than just an address; it's a reflection of the surrounding community, accessibility to amenities, and the overall desirability for potential tenants or buyers. A prime location can not only attract high-quality tenants but also drive demand and appreciation over time.

Data-Driven Decision Making:

In today's digital age, data has emerged as a formidable ally in the realm of real estate investment. Utilizing data analytics and market research tools provides insights into neighborhood dynamics, property values, rental rates, and even the projected future growth of an area. This information empowers investors to make informed decisions that align with their goals and risk tolerance. The ability to access data can also be a downfall. Sometimes there is just so much information you can't take it all in or that information is contradicting. It's important to do the research and find data sources that you can trust and once you find those stick to them. By all means venture out and try others but have core data sources that you trust.

For instance, analyzing historical property values and growth patterns can unveil areas primed for appreciation. Understanding demographic shifts can reveal emerging markets with untapped potential. By harnessing the power of data, investors can capitalize on trends and position themselves ahead of the curve.

Navigating Market Trends:

Market trends act as currents that shape the ebb and flow of the real estate landscape. Being attuned to these trends can mean the difference between an astute investment and a missed opportunity. Economic indicators, consumer behavior, and technological advancements all leave their mark on the market's direction.

Consider the rise of remote work and its impact on housing preferences. As more individuals opt for flexible work arrangements, suburban and rural properties have experienced increased demand. Similarly, understanding the growth of eco-friendly and sustainable practices can guide investments toward properties aligned with evolving consumer values.

Integration into Investment Strategies:

Location and market trends are integral components of a holistic investment strategy. The decision to invest in a particular area should be informed by an analysis of its present attributes, future potential, and alignment with your investment objectives. For example, if your goal is long-term appreciation, targeting areas experiencing infrastructure development and population growth might be prudent.

In the case of rental properties, selecting a location with strong demand drivers—such as proximity to educational institutions, employment hubs, or cultural attractions—can contribute to higher occupancy rates and steady rental income.

Conclusion:

As you learn and tune your own skills on your real estate investment journey, consider location and market trends as your guiding stars. The fusion of comprehensive data analysis, a keen understanding of market dynamics, and a vision for future trends can equip you to make confident decisions that unlock the full potential of your investments. Remember, the path to success in real estate lies not only in bricks and mortar but in the intricate dance between location and the ever-evolving rhythm of market trends.

Chapter 2:
Charting the Course:
Financial Readiness and Setting Investment Goals

Before stepping onto the exhilarating path of real estate investment, it's crucial to conduct a comprehensive self-assessment of your financial health and readiness. This introspective journey is akin to laying the foundation of a sturdy structure, ensuring that your investment endeavors are built on a solid and sustainable base. In this section, we delve into the key elements that compose your financial readiness, equipping you with the knowledge to make informed decisions and embark on your real estate journey with confidence.

The Pillars of Financial Health:

Your financial well-being serves as the bedrock for any investment endeavor, and real estate is no exception. Several key factors contribute to your financial health, each of which warrants careful consideration:

Debt-to-Income Ratio (DTI): This ratio, expressed as a percentage, compares your monthly debt payments to your gross monthly income. Lenders use DTI to assess your ability to manage additional debt from a mortgage. A lower DTI indicates a healthier financial position.

Credit Score: A credit score is a numeric representation of your creditworthiness. It plays a pivotal role in securing favorable interest rates for loans. Monitoring and improving your credit score can yield substantial financial benefits.

Capital and Down Payments: Adequate capital reserves and a substantial down payment are essential for real estate investment.

These funds cover initial expenses and serve as a safety net for unforeseen challenges.

Navigating Credit Scores and Interest Rates:

Your credit score acts as a financial fingerprint, influencing the terms of loans and mortgages you may pursue. A higher credit score often translates to lower interest rates, potentially saving you thousands of dollars over the life of a loan. Monitoring your credit score, rectifying errors, and implementing prudent financial habits can contribute to a more favorable credit profile. Did you know that the top three major credit scores that banks pull also use FICO. But they can also pull any of the 16 FICO scores that play a role into your credit worthiness as well? Yeah 16 official FICO scores!

FICO® Score 2: Mortgage lenders get this version of the FICO® Score from Experian.

FICO® Score 4: Mortgage lenders get this version of the FICO® Score from TransUnion.

FICO® Score 5: Mortgage lenders obtain this version of the FICO® Score from Equifax.

And 13 others....

Self-Assessment and Market Knowledge:

Investing in real estate demands a degree of market acumen. Self-assess your familiarity with real estate dynamics, including property values, rental rates, and local market trends. Establish clear investment goals that align with your risk tolerance and financial objectives. For instance, pinpoint milestones like accumulating a specific amount of capital or achieving a certain credit score before embarking on your investment journey.

Knowing When You're Ready:

Recognizing your readiness to invest involves a comprehensive evaluation of your financial landscape and a pragmatic understanding of your real estate aspirations. Ask yourself key questions:

- Do I have a solid grasp of my financial situation?
- Is my credit score in a range that will secure favorable loan terms?
- Do I possess the necessary capital and down payment funds?
- Am I familiar with the local real estate market and its trends?
- Have I set clear investment goals and milestones?

By answering these questions honestly and objectively, you'll gain a clearer perspective on your readiness to dive into the world of real estate investment. Remember, readiness is not solely a financial matter; it's also about equipping yourself with the knowledge and preparation to navigate the complexities of the real estate market.

Setting Clear Investment Goals and Objectives

In the realm of real estate investment, a compass is as vital as a map. Setting clear and well-defined investment goals serves as your guiding compass, ensuring that your journey is purposeful, strategic, and aligned with your financial aspirations. In this section, we'll delve into the art of crafting effective investment goals and provide you with a comprehensive checklist to refer back to as you embark on your real estate venture.

Define Your Purpose: Begin by outlining your overarching purpose for investing in real estate. Are you seeking long-term wealth accumulation, supplemental income, or retirement security? Your purpose will shape the trajectory of your investment strategy.

Quantify Your Objectives: Set specific, measurable, achievable, relevant, and time-bound (SMART) objectives. For instance, aim to acquire three rental properties within the next five years, generating a monthly passive income of $5,000.

Risk Tolerance: Gauge your risk tolerance level. Are you comfortable with higher-risk, higher-reward ventures, or do you prefer more conservative investments? Understanding your risk profile will help you select the right investment opportunities.

Property Type and Market: Determine whether you want to focus on residential, commercial, or industrial properties. Research and select target markets based on factors like population growth, employment opportunities, and property demand.

Cash Flow Goals: Specify your desired cash flow. Calculate the monthly income you aim to generate from your real estate investments after deducting expenses like mortgage payments, maintenance, and property management.

Equity Growth: Outline your expectations for equity growth over time. How much appreciation do you anticipate your properties will experience, and over what period?

Portfolio Diversification: Consider how you'll diversify your portfolio to mitigate risks. Determine the ideal mix of property types, locations, and investment strategies.

Exit Strategy: Define your exit strategy for each property. Will you sell after a certain period, refinance, or continue holding for long-term income?

Financing and Leverage: Set goals for leveraging your investments. How much of your own capital are you willing to invest, and how much financing will you seek?

Education and Research: Commit to ongoing education and research. Regularly update your knowledge of market trends, property management practices, legal regulations, and financial strategies.

Your Investment Goal Checklist:

Purpose: Is my investment purpose clearly defined?

Specificity: Are my investment objectives specific and measurable?

Risk Tolerance: Have I assessed my risk tolerance and aligned it with my goals?

Property Focus: Have I chosen a property type and market that align with my objectives?

Cash Flow: Have I determined the desired cash flow from my investments?

Equity Growth: What are my expectations for property appreciation and equity growth?

Diversification: Have I planned for portfolio diversification?

Exit Strategy: Is there a clear exit strategy for each property?

Leverage: Have I decided on the level of financing and leverage I'll use?

Education: Am I committed to continuous education and research?

By methodically addressing each point on this investment goal checklist, you'll equip yourself with a robust framework for success. Your investment goals will serve as a dynamic compass, guiding your decisions, actions, and endeavors in the exciting world of real estate investment. As you chart your course toward financial prosperity, these goals will ensure that you remain on track, adapt to changing conditions, and ultimately arrive at your desired destination.

Creating a Comprehensive Investment Plan: Transforming Goals into Action

Crafting well-defined investment goals is like architecting the blueprint for a grand building. However, turning these aspirations into reality requires a comprehensive investment plan that outlines the specific steps, strategies, and timelines needed to achieve each goal. In this section, we'll guide you through the process of translating your investment goals into a practical and actionable plan that propels you toward real estate success.

Step 1: Goal Refinement

Review and refine your investment goals. Ensure they are clear, realistic, and aligned with your financial aspirations. Seek to balance your risk tolerance, desired returns, and investment time horizon.

Step 2: Property Type and Market Research

Based on your property focus, conduct thorough research on target markets. Analyze factors such as population trends, employment growth, rental demand, and property appreciation rates. Identify areas that align with your investment objectives.

Step 3: Property Acquisition Strategy

Determine the most suitable property acquisition strategy for your goals. Are you aiming for rental income, property appreciation, or a mix of both? Decide whether you'll invest in single-family homes, multifamily properties, commercial spaces, or a combination.

Step 4: Financing and Leverage

Evaluate your financing options and leverage strategy. Determine how much of your own capital you'll invest and explore various mortgage options. Calculate the potential loan-to-value ratios and estimate monthly mortgage payments.

Step 5: Property Selection Criteria

Establish clear criteria for property selection. Define the minimum cash flow, equity growth potential, and market conditions you require. Create a checklist to evaluate potential properties against your criteria.

Step 6: Due Diligence and Risk Assessment

Perform thorough due diligence on potential properties. Inspect physical conditions, review property histories, and assess local market risks. Factor in potential repair costs and vacancy rates when calculating your projected returns.

Step 7: Property Management Strategy

Decide whether you'll manage the properties yourself or hire a property management company. Outline property management responsibilities, tenant screening procedures, and maintenance plans.

Step 8: Exit Strategies

Detail your exit strategies for each property. Determine triggers for selling, refinancing, or holding based on market conditions, equity growth, and your overall financial goals.

Step 9: Financial Projections

Create detailed financial projections for each investment. Estimate cash flow, equity growth, and potential tax implications. Use these projections to assess the feasibility of your investment plan.

Step 10: Monitoring and Reevaluation

Set regular intervals to monitor your investments' performance. Reevaluate your investment plan annually or when market conditions change. Adjust your strategies based on real-time data and evolving goals.

Step 11: Ongoing Education

Commit to continuous learning and education in the real estate field. Stay informed about market trends, legal updates, and best practices to make informed decisions.

Step 12: Seek Professional Guidance

Consider seeking advice from financial advisors, real estate professionals, and mentors. Their expertise can provide valuable insights and help refine your investment plan.

By systematically converting your investment goals into an actionable plan, you transform abstract ambitions into concrete steps toward financial prosperity. This comprehensive investment plan becomes your roadmap, guiding you through the dynamic landscape of real estate investment. As you execute each step, track your progress and make adjustments as needed. With dedication, diligence, and a well-structured plan, you'll navigate the complexities of real estate investment with confidence, working steadily toward the achievement of your goals.

Chapter 3:
Navigating the Real Estate Market

One of the cornerstones of successful real estate investment is the diligent research and analysis that precedes any decision-making. To make informed and calculated investment choices, it's essential to conduct comprehensive market research and due diligence. In this section, we'll delve into the key steps and strategies for conducting effective research, accessing valuable information, and utilizing tools like real estate investment calculators.

Step 1: Defining Your Investment Criteria

Before you embark on market research, establish your investment criteria. Determine the property type, location, expected returns, and risk tolerance that align with your goals. Having clear criteria will help you narrow down your focus and streamline your research efforts.

Step 2: Identifying Reliable Data Sources

Accessing accurate and reliable data is crucial for informed decision-making. Utilize a combination of online resources, government databases, real estate market reports, and local economic indicators. Websites like Zillow, Realtor.com, Redfin, and local MLS platforms provide up-to-date property listings, historical sales data, and market trends.

Step 3: Analyzing Local Market Trends

Study the local market dynamics by analyzing factors such as population growth, employment rates, rental demand, and property appreciation trends. Look for emerging neighborhoods with potential for value appreciation. Research local amenities, schools, transportation, and future development plans that can impact property values.

Step 4: Building a Real Estate Investment Calculator

A real estate investment calculator is a powerful tool for analyzing potential investments. You can use online calculators or create your own customized spreadsheet. Input variables like property price, down payment, mortgage terms, property taxes, insurance, maintenance costs, and potential rental income. The calculator will provide insights into cash flow, return on investment (ROI), and other financial metrics.

Step 5: Assessing Property Condition

Conduct thorough due diligence on individual properties of interest. Inspect physical conditions, identify potential repair costs, and assess any needed renovations. Examine property histories, including past sales, ownership changes, and any legal or zoning issues.

Step 6: Evaluating Comparable Properties

Compare your chosen property with similar properties in the area. Look at recent sales prices, rental rates, and occupancy rates. This analysis helps you determine whether the property is priced competitively and aligns with market trends.

Step 7: Networking and Local Insights

Engage with local real estate professionals, agents, investors, and property managers. They can provide valuable insights into the local market conditions, upcoming developments, and investment opportunities. Attend real estate seminars, workshops, and networking events to expand your knowledge and contacts.

Step 8: Continuous Monitoring and Adaptation

Market conditions are dynamic, so it's important to continuously monitor trends and adapt your strategies accordingly. Regularly revisit your market research and due diligence process to stay updated on changes that may impact your investment decisions.

By diligently conducting market research and due diligence, you empower yourself with the information needed to make sound investment choices. Leveraging tools like real estate investment calculators streamlines your analysis and provides a clear financial picture of potential investments. Remember that successful real estate investing requires a blend of data-driven analysis, local insights, and a forward-looking mindset. With each step you take to understand the market, you move closer to building a robust real estate portfolio that aligns with your investment objectives.

Property cycles, a fundamental aspect of real estate investment, are the rhythmic patterns that shape the market's fluctuations over time. These cycles follow a recurring sequence of stages, each characterized by unique trends and conditions. By comprehending the dynamics of property cycles and honing your ability to analyze economic indicators, you can make informed investment decisions and position yourself for success in the ever-evolving real estate landscape.

Decoding the Phases of Property Cycles

Property cycles typically consist of four distinct phases:

Recovery: This phase marks the turnaround from a downturn, with declining vacancy rates, stabilizing prices, and increased demand. It's a period of cautious optimism, often characterized by limited construction activity.

Expansion: As the market gains momentum, this phase witnesses rising demand, increased construction, and growing property values. Rental rates tend to rise, and investors experience healthy returns.

Hyper-Supply: During this phase, the market becomes saturated with new developments, leading to higher vacancy rates and slowing price growth. Rent growth might stall, and investors need to exercise caution.

Recession: The culmination of a cycle, this phase is characterized by falling demand, declining prices, and higher vacancies. Investors should prepare for reduced returns, and opportunities arise for those with available capital.

Analyzing Economic Indicators:

Economic indicators provide essential insights into the health of a market and potential shifts in property cycles. These indicators include:

Employment Rates: A strong job market drives demand for housing and rental properties. Monitoring employment data can help you gauge market vitality.

Population Growth: Growing populations often lead to increased housing demand, potentially indicating an upswing in the property cycle.

Interest Rates: Fluctuating interest rates influence borrowing costs and affordability, impacting both property demand and value.

Consumer Confidence: Positive consumer sentiment can drive spending and investment, influencing the real estate market's performance.

Supply and Demand: Balancing the ratio of available properties and potential tenants is crucial for understanding market conditions.

Responding to Property Cycles:

Understanding property cycles empowers investors to adjust their strategies accordingly:

Acquisition Timing: Identify the phase of the cycle to make informed decisions about when to buy, hold, or sell properties.

Risk Management: Recognize that each phase presents unique risks and opportunities. Diversification and due diligence become crucial tools for mitigating risk.

Strategic Planning: Align your investment goals with the prevailing phase of the cycle. For example, focus on income-generating properties during downturns and consider development opportunities during upswings.

Long-Term Vision: Recognize that property cycles are cyclical, and a long-term perspective can help you weather short-term fluctuations.

Market Research: Continuously analyze economic indicators to stay ahead of market shifts and position yourself advantageously.

Navigating the property landscape requires a combination of historical understanding, diligent research, and adaptability. By mastering the nuances of property cycles and economic indicators, you equip yourself with a robust toolkit for thriving in the ever-changing world of real estate investment. Through informed decision-making and strategic planning, you can confidently set sail on your investment journey, guided by the steady compass of property cycles.

Recognizing emerging market trends is akin to unveiling the future landscape. A market trend denotes the prevailing direction of a market's movement over time. Analyzing these trends is a fundamental skill that allows investors to anticipate shifts, adapt strategies, and seize lucrative opportunities. By delving into the art and science of identifying market trends, you can position yourself to harness the potential of the ever-evolving real estate market.

So let's discuss understanding market trends

Market trends encompass the overarching patterns in supply, demand, and pricing within a specific geographic area or property type. These trends can span various durations, from short-term fluctuations to long-term shifts. Identifying and interpreting these trends equips investors with insights into potential risks and rewards.

Identifying Market Trends

There are several tools and techniques that can aid in the identification of market trends and as the goal with this book is to give you information to start we will get into a few specifics.

Data Analysis: In the digital age, data has become a powerful tool. Analyze historical sales, rental, and price data to discern patterns and potential shifts.

Comparative Market Analysis (CMA): CMAs evaluate recent property sales and listings to determine property values and gauge market demand.

Local Economic Indicators: Factors such as job growth, population changes, and infrastructure development can influence market trends.

Real Estate Investment Calculators: These tools help assess potential returns on investments and can aid in predicting market shifts.

Recognizing emerging market trends holds paramount significance for real estate investment strategies.

Informed Decision-Making: Investors armed with trend insights can make informed decisions regarding property acquisition, rental rates, and potential appreciation.

Risk Mitigation: Identifying market shifts early allows investors to adjust strategies, reducing exposure to potential downturns.

Capitalizing on Opportunities: Emerging trends often signify untapped opportunities. By identifying these trends, investors can position themselves to seize favorable conditions. Are new schools being built? That is a great indicator of money and growth.

Portfolio Optimization: Understanding market trends aids in optimizing portfolio diversification, balancing investments across different property types and geographic locations.

Effective utilization of market trends involves aligning investment strategies with emerging opportunities.

Adaptive Strategies: Tailor investment strategies based on current and projected market trends to optimize returns.

Long-Term Vision: While trends can offer short-term benefits, an overarching long-term vision ensures sustainable investment success. For example, if your goal is to invest for your retirement and you're in your early 30s, market trend isn't going to be as important because trends can be on a 15 to 20 year cycle. Which means the one that you're studying now will likely not be the one that you'll be utilizing when you retire.

Location-Centric Approach: Geography plays a pivotal role in market trends. Evaluate local trends to devise strategies tailored to specific markets. I am of the opinion that you should invest within 30 to 40 minutes of driving time from your home. This is because you know this area do you know people in this area and you are investments will be more easily managed.

Data-Driven Decisions: Leverage data and analytical tools to validate trends, ensuring well-informed decisions.

Mastering the art of identifying emerging market trends is akin to foreseeing the winds of change. By studying historical data, employing analytical tools, and understanding economic indicators, investors can chart a course that aligns with the evolving real estate landscape. The ability to discern trends and seize emerging opportunities empowers investors to harness the full potential of their investment journey, guiding them toward prosperous horizons amidst the dynamic currents of the real estate market.

In the ever-evolving world of real estate investment, the year 2023 has brought forth a significant shift in market dynamics. Gone are the days of a uniform national trajectory that propelled property values skyward. Instead, a more nuanced, regionally-diverse landscape has emerged, necessitating a refined approach to investment strategy. This shift marks a departure from the era when investing in real estate seemed straightforward due to a nationwide wave of momentum.

The Dawn of Regional Evaluation:

In the recent past, a surge in real estate values appeared to be a shared phenomenon across the entire nation. Investors could often rely on a rising tide that lifted all markets. However, 2023 has introduced a new reality—one where the momentum has subsided and distinct regional trends have emerged. Now, understanding local market nuances has become paramount.

Varied Trajectories Across the Nation:

As we stand in 2023, the real estate landscape paints a picture of diversity:

Climbing Heights: In certain regions, property values continue their upward ascent. Robust local economies, population growth, and limited supply have sustained the upward trajectory. These areas offer potential for continued appreciation and attractive investment prospects.

Steady Ground: Other locales have experienced a stabilization of property values. Economic indicators and population trends have harmonized, resulting in a balanced market with steady but moderate growth. These regions provide reliability for investors seeking stability.

Falling Short: In contrast, some markets have faced challenges leading to a decline in property values. Economic setbacks, oversupply, or shifting demographics have contributed to diminished investor returns. Navigating these areas requires heightened caution.

A Paradigm Shift for Investors:

The shift from a national to a regional evaluation model signals a paradigm shift for real estate investors. The one-size-fits-all approach of yesteryears no longer suffices. Instead, savvy investors must tailor their strategies to the specificities of each region. This shift highlights the importance of granular market knowledge, local economic indicators, and demographic trends.

Navigating the New Landscape:

Market Research Reinvented: Instead of relying solely on national trends, diligent investors now delve into localized market research. Understanding the pulse of a specific region is vital for accurate decision-making. There are many cities around the United States that on sixth Street and you can have high property values high demand for housing but on seventh and fifth Street prices can drop dramatically because that street is not highly desired.

Adaptive Strategies: Investment strategies must now adapt to the unique demands of each region. A one-size-fits-all approach is replaced by a nimble strategy that considers regional supply and demand dynamics. As mentioned before finding comparables is important because you would think you could use a comparable one street over but there might be a small nuance difference that makes one street over a higher demand versus the other. These are small things that an investor that is not investing in their local market would not know.

Mitigating Risks: Recognizing markets that are slowing down or experiencing a decline helps investors mitigate risks. Diligence in risk assessment and careful property selection is paramount. Using recent home sales, poverty rate, unemployment rate, and new jobs listings within your investment area are good ways to weigh the risks for investing

Seizing Opportunities: While some regions present challenges, they also offer untapped potential. Investors with a discerning eye can uncover opportunities amidst the shifts.

Conclusion: Navigating the Regionally-Charged Waters

The transformation from a nationwide wave of momentum to a regionally-diverse landscape marks a pivotal juncture in the real estate investment journey. In 2023 and beyond, astute investors recognize that national trends no longer tell the complete story. By embracing localized insights, adapting strategies, and seizing opportunities within each distinct region, investors are well-equipped to navigate the regionally-charged waters and capitalize on the unique opportunities that this new era presents.

Chapter 4:
Weaving the Threads of Financial Foundation:
Funding Your Real Estate Journey

Exploring Various Financing Options: Mortgages, Loans, Partnerships, and More

Understanding the array of financing options at your disposal is essential. This section delves into the most popular financing methods, providing insights into their requirements, down payment considerations, equity necessities, and the strategic significance of each.

Mortgages: Tailoring Your Debt to Investment Objectives

A mortgage, a cornerstone of real estate financing, allows investors to secure a property by borrowing a portion of its value while committing a down payment. The type of mortgage you choose can significantly impact your investment strategy. This is because the mortgage type that you select can add fees and monthly costs that contribute to your business expenses, changing the operating income.

Conventional Mortgages: Typically offered by banks and other financial institutions, conventional mortgages are secured by the property itself. Requirements often include a favorable credit score, stable income, and a down payment ranging from 5% to 20% of the property's purchase price. Higher down payments can lead to lower interest rates and may reduce the need for private mortgage insurance (PMI) when down payments are less than 20%. With a conventional mortgage if you have PMI you will pay that premium until your value is above 20% of the home value. In this sense your value would mean the equity that you have in the house. A conventional mortgage allows for more flexibility when it comes to loan options. You have the option to buy down your interest rate, through points, at times this can be expensive but advantageous and other times it's not worth it. You will need to run the numbers and check your math before doing so.

FHA Loans: Backed by the Federal Housing Administration, FHA loans offer a more accessible path for first-time investors. These loans require a lower down payment—usually around 3.5%—and may be more lenient toward credit history. While this avenue provides an entry point for investors with limited upfront capital, it's important to note that FHA loans require private mortgage insurance (PMI) throughout the loan term. This differs from a conventional loan because once you have 20% Equity with an FHA loan the PMI does not automatically get removed.

Portfolio Loans: Offered by some banks, portfolio loans provide greater flexibility in underwriting criteria. This option might be suitable for investors with unconventional financial profiles or those seeking to finance multiple properties under one loan.

Collaborative Ventures:

In real estate investment, partnerships can amplify your financial capacity and pool resources to tackle larger and more lucrative projects. Investors often opt for partnerships when they aim to diversify their investment portfolios, share financial burdens, or tap into specialized expertise. Partnerships can be a great way to increase your purchasing power allowing you to invest in larger properties. However, with partnerships, they come with different opinions on how things should operate, how money should be spent etc. In most cases the people you would partner with bring a specific skill, are more knowledgeable than you are on certain topics and their input is valuable. In other cases some people feel that because they have money invested they should have full say in how things operate this can create turmoil within the investment. Just as you would research a property before buying it, you should research an investor before partnering with them. There are also silent partners and active partners. You can stipulate in the agreement which type of partner you are looking for or what type of partner the investor would like to be. A silent partner would be someone who brings money to the table and expects a certain amount of return but does not work on a day-to-day basis like an active partner would. They are not in all the decisions and sometimes they make no decisions at all.

Joint Ventures: Two or more investors join forces to finance and manage a real estate project. This approach leverages the strengths of each partner and spreads risk across multiple shoulders.

Limited Partnerships: In this structure, general partners manage the investment and decision-making, while limited partners contribute capital. Limited partners enjoy potential returns without being actively involved in management.

Equity Partnerships: Partnerships can also manifest as equity-sharing arrangements, where investors share ownership in a property. This approach can allow for creative financing, reduced capital requirements, and the division of responsibilities.

Bridge Loans and Hard Money Loans:

For investors seeking short-term financing to seize time-sensitive opportunities, bridge loans and hard money loans offer solutions. These loans are often used to secure properties for renovation, resale, or refinancing. It's important to understand that these types of loans are short-term and bring a higher risk which typically means a higher interest rate. So when you're investing and using these types of loans it's best to use them and get them paid back as fast as you can .

Bridge Loans: Bridge loans provide temporary financing, typically for periods ranging from a few months to a few years. They can help investors secure properties before obtaining long-term financing.

Hard Money Loans: These loans are asset-based and focus on the value of the property being acquired. While hard money loans may have higher interest rates, they can be valuable for investors who need quick access to capital or have less-than-perfect credit.

Calculating Financial Feasibility and Return on Investment (ROI)

Success is often determined by your ability to analyze and quantify the potential returns of a property. This section delves into the five most important calculations that form the bedrock of financial feasibility assessment and provide a clear understanding of your investment's potential. These calculations not only help you evaluate the viability of a property but also play a crucial role in shaping your overall investment strategy. Lets go over what I believe to be the 5 most important calculations when determining if a property is worth its salt.

1. Gross Rental Yield

Calculation: Gross Rental Yield = (Annual Rental Income / Property Purchase Price) × 100

The gross rental yield provides a quick snapshot of a property's income-generating potential. It highlights the proportion of rental income relative to the property's cost. A higher gross rental yield indicates better potential for cash flow, making it a valuable tool for initial screening.

2. Net Operating Income (NOI)

Calculation: NOI = Gross Rental Income - Operating Expenses

The net operating income assesses the profitability of an income-producing property after accounting for operating costs. A positive NOI indicates that the property generates sufficient income to cover expenses, suggesting its financial viability.

3. Cash-on-Cash Return

Calculation: Cash-on-Cash Return = (Annual Pre-Tax Cash Flow / Total Cash Investment) × 100

Cash-on-cash return reveals the percentage return on your actual investment, considering both cash flow and initial cash investment. This metric helps you understand the annual return relative to the money you've invested.

4. Return on Investment (ROI)

Calculation: ROI = (Total Gain from Investment - Total Cost of Investment) / Total Cost of Investment

Return on investment measures the profitability of a property, factoring in all gains and costs. It provides a comprehensive overview of your financial performance and guides you in comparing different investment opportunities.

5. Cap Rate (Capitalization Rate)

Calculation: Cap Rate = (Net Operating Income / Property Purchase Price) × 100

The cap rate gauges the potential return on a property based on its net operating income and purchase price. It serves as a benchmark for evaluating the income-generating capacity of a property and helps you compare similar properties in different markets.

Each of these calculations contributes a unique perspective to your real estate investment analysis. While gross rental yield and cap rate provide insight into the property's income potential and market value, NOI and cash-on-cash return focus on financial feasibility and cash flow. ROI offers a comprehensive overview of your profitability, factoring in all aspects of your investment. These calculations together create a holistic understanding of your potential returns, ensuring that you make well-informed investment decisions that align with your financial goals.

Managing Leverage and Mitigating Risks

It's essential to recognize that while the potential for lucrative returns is significant, the associated risks require careful consideration and management. This final section of Chapter Four explores how you can effectively manage leverage and mitigate risks to ensure a sustainable and successful real estate investment journey.

Understanding the Role of Leverage:

Leverage, the strategic use of borrowed capital to increase the potential return on investment, can be a powerful tool in real estate. However, it's a double-edged sword that requires prudent management. The earlier sections of this chapter introduced you to various financing options, highlighting how leveraging can amplify returns. Yet, it's crucial to strike a balance between the potential for higher returns and the risk of overextending yourself. If you take on too much risk, or in this case, you borrowed too much money. There are still a monthly payment to be made. There is a potential that ou will go through a period of vacancy. If you are not making money through renting a property or otherwise it falls on you to be able to float the business expenses until you become cash-flow positive again.

Painting the Picture of Risk:
"I will tell you what changed my whole life. I finally discovered it's all risky. If you think trying is risky, wait until they hand you the bill for not trying."
-Jim Rohn

The calculations discussed earlier, such as ROI, cap rate, and cash-on-cash return, are not just numbers; they provide a comprehensive insight into the financial health and potential of a property. They help you gauge the level of risk associated with an investment. High leverage, while magnifying potential gains, can also intensify losses in the event of market downturns or unexpected expenses. Thoroughly analyzing these metrics enables you to assess the feasibility of an investment, guiding you away from properties that might not align with your financial objectives.

The Perils of Over-Leveraging:

While leverage can turbocharge your returns, it's crucial to avoid the pitfall of over-leveraging. High levels of debt can lead to cash flow challenges, making it difficult to cover mortgage payments, maintenance costs, and other expenses. In extreme cases, this could result in foreclosure or forced property sales. By staying mindful of your debt-to-income ratio, you can strike a balance that ensures sustainable cash flow and protects your long-term financial stability.

Knowing When to Walk Away:

Not every property will be a lucrative investment, and that's perfectly acceptable. In the pursuit of attractive opportunities, it's important to acknowledge that some properties might not meet your investment criteria or offer the desired returns. Thorough market research, due diligence, and financial analysis empower you to recognize when it's time to walk away from a potential investment, safeguarding your resources and preserving your financial well-being.

Diversification as a Risk Mitigation Strategy:

Diversifying your real estate portfolio across different property types, locations, and investment strategies is a proven approach to mitigating risk. By spreading your investments, you reduce your exposure to downturns in a single market or asset class. This strategy can help safeguard your portfolio's stability and maintain a consistent level of income even during challenging economic conditions.

In the dynamic world of real estate investing, managing leverage and mitigating risks is an ongoing process. It requires vigilance, a clear understanding of your financial capabilities, and a willingness to adjust your strategy when necessary. By mastering the art of risk management and making informed decisions, you position yourself for long-term success in the rewarding realm of real estate investment. Remember, a well-managed investment journey isn't just about chasing high returns; it's about ensuring sustainable growth and financial security.

Chapter 5:
Residential Real Estate Investments

Strategies for Investing in Single-Family Homes, Duplexes, and Condos

In residential real estate investments, a multitude of strategies can be employed to capitalize on the opportunities presented by single-family homes, duplexes, and condos. Let's delve into some of the most effective strategies, each offering a unique avenue to achieve your investment goals.

1. House Hacking: Maximizing Returns Through Strategic Living

What Is House Hacking? House hacking involves purchasing a multi-unit property, such as a duplex or triplex, or quadplex and living in one unit while renting out the others. This strategy allows you to cover your living expenses with rental income.

How to Get Started: Utilizing FHA Loans for Multifamily House Hacking

One highly advantageous approach to embarking on your house hacking journey is by taking advantage of Federal Housing Administration (FHA) loans. These loans offer an excellent opportunity for investors looking to purchase a multifamily property they intend to live in, enabling them to secure financing with as little as 3.5% down.

Identifying Multifamily Properties: Your first step involves identifying suitable multifamily properties in desirable neighborhoods. Look for duplexes, triplexes, or four-unit buildings that align with your investment goals and offer the potential for rental income from the additional units.

Calculating Potential Rental Income: Once you've found a promising multifamily property, calculate the potential rental income from the additional units. Research local rental rates for similar properties to estimate how much you can reasonably charge for rent. This projected rental income will be a key factor in determining the feasibility of covering a significant portion of your mortgage through house hacking.

Determining Mortgage Feasibility: One of the primary advantages of utilizing an FHA loan for house hacking is the minimal down payment requirement. With as little as 3.5% down, you can secure financing for the multifamily property. This reduced upfront investment allows you to preserve your capital for other aspects of your investment strategy. However it's important to note that with only 3.5% down your monthly payment will be higher than if you were to have put a larger down payment towards the purchase.

FHA Loan Benefits: FHA loans offer a range of benefits for investors pursuing house hacking. These include competitive interest rates, lenient credit requirements, and the ability to finance both the property purchase and potential renovation costs.

House Hacking Advantage: By utilizing an FHA loan, you're leveraging the power of house hacking to not only reduce your own living costs but also to kickstart your real estate investment journey. The rental income from the additional units can offset a significant portion of your mortgage payment, making it a financially savvy decision.

Residency Requirement: It's important to note that FHA loans come with a residency requirement. You must live in one of the units as your primary residence for at least one year. This requirement aligns with the house hacking strategy and provides you with the opportunity to experience firsthand the benefits and challenges of being a landlord.

Building Your Portfolio: Once you've successfully house hacked your first multifamily property using an FHA loan, you'll have gained valuable experience as an investor and landlord. As you build equity and your financial situation improves, you may choose to repeat the process, acquiring additional multifamily properties and expanding your real estate portfolio.

Let's make up an example to see how a multi-family investment using an FHA loan can get you started in investing in real estate. Let's use a $200,000 purchase price for a Triplex that you intend to live in one unit.

This would mean that to come to close, you would need to bring $7,000 in a down payment and lets estimate about $5,000 in closing costs. This means all in, you will need to bring $12,000 to purchase a $200,000 house.

Just for simplicity we are going to round these numbers.
Your loan options for an FHA loan would look something similar to $200,000 purchase - $7,000 down payment, Meaning your loan amount would be $197,000. If we apply a 2023 interest rate of 7%, we get a monthly payment of roughly $1,300. However this does not include insurance or taxes or PMI. We sum these added thing as a total PITI (Principal, Interest, Taxes, Insurance) + PMI. With all these things added our new monthly payment would be around $1,800 a month.

Now let's assume that we can get $800 a month from each unit we are not intending to live in as this is a Triplex that means we will be making $1,600 per month. Assume a 25% loss on that monthly income for repairs, maintenance, vacancies, etc, etc. This brings our total monthly income to $1,200 per month. If you are to apply that to your monthly payment for your mortgage that would mean you could own a Triplex worth $200,000 for roughly $600 a month while setting aside 25% for repairs and maintenance of the building.

2. Saving and Investing: Building Wealth Over Time

What Is Saving and Investing? This strategy involves diligently saving money over time to accumulate the funds needed for a down payment on a single-family home. Over time, you can leverage your initial investment to acquire additional properties.

Creating a Budget and Savings Strategy: Begin by thoroughly assessing your current financial status. Devise a comprehensive budget that designates a specific portion of your income for real estate investments. Cultivate a disciplined savings approach that will enable you to accumulate the necessary capital to enter the real estate market.

Exploring Mortgage Options and Property Prices: Immerse yourself in researching the range of mortgage options available to you. While FHA loans offer an appealing route for properties intended for your residence for at least 12 months, be mindful that they have residency requirements. Should you be considering investment properties that don't adhere to this criterion, alternative financing avenues will be essential.

Understanding Investment Property Requirements: As you venture into the realm of investment properties, it's imperative to grasp the baseline requisites set forth by financial institutions. On average, a 20% down payment is typically expected for investment properties. Moreover, banks may stipulate the maintenance of a cash reserve equivalent to six months of operating expenses (OPEX) to ensure financial stability and readiness.

You can use the same example above and change your down payment amount to be 20% and no PMI while living in the third unit of the triplex and you can see how it adjusts your profit margins. You can use that same math to extrapolate further, that you can rent all three units for $800 a month and then see how this property would be cash flow positive.

3. Owner Financing: Creating Win-Win Deals

What Is Owner Financing? In this strategy, you negotiate with the property owner to finance the purchase directly. Instead of obtaining a traditional mortgage from a bank, you make monthly payments to the seller.

Understanding Seller Financing: Seller financing, also known as owner financing, involves entering into an agreement with the property seller to secure financing directly from them. This arrangement bypasses traditional lending institutions and allows you to negotiate terms directly with the seller. The terms of the financing, including interest rates, repayment schedules, and down payment structures, are established through a formal agreement.

Key Benefits of Seller Financing:

Accessible Financing: Seller financing can be an attractive option for individuals who may not meet the stringent criteria of conventional lenders.

Flexible Terms: Negotiating directly with the seller provides an opportunity to tailor financing terms that align with your investment strategy.

Streamlined Process: Seller financing often results in a faster and more straightforward closing process compared to traditional bank loans.

Important Considerations:

Interest Rates: It's important to note that seller financing typically comes with higher interest rates compared to traditional mortgage rates.

Financial Analysis: Conduct a comprehensive financial analysis, including Return on Investment (ROI) and Capitalization Rate (Cap Rate) calculations, to determine the viability of the investment under the proposed terms.

Long-Term Implications: While seller financing can offer advantages, ensure that you thoroughly understand the long-term financial implications of the arrangement.

Calculating ROI and Cap Rate: ROI = [(Net Profit / Total Investment) × 100] Cap Rate = (Net Operating Income / Property Value) × 100

By considering seller financing, you can potentially unlock investment opportunities that may have been otherwise unavailable. This strategy underscores the importance of thorough financial analysis and due diligence to ensure that the terms align with your investment goals and contribute to your long-term success in the world of real estate.

4.Exploring Real Estate Investment Trusts (REITs): A Passive Income Avenue

Understanding REITs: Real Estate Investment Trusts (REITs) present a dynamic opportunity for individuals seeking exposure to the real estate market without the complexities of property ownership. Essentially, REITs function as investment vehicles that own, manage, or finance income-generating properties, such as commercial, residential, or industrial real estate. By investing in REITs, you become a shareholder in a diversified portfolio of properties, offering potential benefits and income streams.

Investment Channels and Benefits: Investing in REITs offers various pathways for participation. You can explore publicly-traded REITs, which are listed on stock exchanges and provide ease of access through brokerage accounts. Alternatively, private REITs are accessible through financial advisors and provide an avenue for a more tailored investment approach.

One notable allure of REITs is the potential for attractive dividend yields. REITs are mandated to distribute a significant portion of their earnings as dividends to shareholders, often resulting in higher dividend yields compared to other investment options. These dividends can serve as a consistent income stream, making REITs particularly appealing for investors seeking passive income.

Risk Considerations: While REITs offer enticing income potential, it's essential to acknowledge certain risks. The value of REIT investments can be influenced by factors such as interest rate fluctuations, economic conditions, and changes in property market dynamics. Additionally, the value of REIT shares may not always correlate with traditional stock market movements.

REIT Dividends and Taxation: REIT dividends differ from typical stock dividends. REIT dividends are considered "qualified dividends" and are subject to a unique taxation structure. They are generally taxed at the individual's ordinary income tax rate, potentially higher than the favorable tax rate for qualified stock dividends. Investors should consult with tax professionals to understand the tax implications specific to their situation.

The Passive Income Advantage: Investing in REITs offers a remarkable avenue for generating passive income. Unlike active property ownership, where responsibilities include property management and maintenance, REIT investors can enjoy a hands-off approach. This makes REITs an optimal choice for those seeking income without the demands of day-to-day property management.

The Power of Research and Evaluation: While REITs can be a compelling investment, it's crucial to engage in thorough research before committing capital. Evaluate the REIT's historical performance, management team, property portfolio, and financial health. Regularly reevaluate your investment to ensure it aligns with your financial goals and market conditions.

Incorporating REITs into your investment strategy presents an opportunity to partake in real estate's potential for passive income, diversification, and potential growth. By understanding the nuances of REIT investments and conducting diligent research, you can navigate the realm of REITs with confidence and set the stage for a steady stream of income in your investment journey.

5. Exploring Room Renting: Meeting Shared Housing Demand

Understanding Room Renting: The strategy of renting out individual rooms within a single-family home taps into a burgeoning trend of shared housing. This approach involves purchasing a residential property and leasing separate rooms to tenants, capitalizing on the rising demand for affordable and communal living spaces, particularly among young professionals and students.

The Significance of Lease Agreements: When venturing into room renting, having comprehensive and well-drafted lease agreements is paramount. Lease agreements outline the terms and conditions of the rental arrangement, protecting both landlords and tenants. These documents detail crucial aspects such as rent amounts, payment schedules, house rules, responsibilities, and termination clauses. A clearly defined lease agreement fosters a transparent and harmonious living environment while mitigating potential conflicts.

Risk Management and Safety Considerations: While room renting presents income opportunities, it's crucial to be aware of the associated risks. Sharing a living space with multiple individuals may introduce challenges related to tenant interactions, shared responsibilities, and property maintenance. Tenant turnover can also be higher in shared housing scenarios. To mitigate these risks, thorough tenant screening and reference checks are essential. Additionally, establishing house rules and conducting periodic inspections can help maintain order and upkeep.

Short-Term and Long-Term Rental Options: Room renting offers versatility in terms of rental durations. You can choose between short-term and long-term rental arrangements based on market demand and your investment goals. Short-term rentals, which may include vacation stays or temporary housing solutions, can yield higher rental income but require more active management. Long-term rentals, on the other hand, offer stability and predictable income, often preferred by students or professionals seeking stable housing arrangements.

Emphasizing Safety and Security: Safety concerns are of paramount importance when renting out individual rooms. Landlords should prioritize the safety of their tenants by implementing security measures such as secure locks, smoke detectors, and emergency contact information. Adequate insurance coverage, including liability insurance, is essential to safeguard against unforeseen events.

Navigating the Regulatory Landscape: Depending on your location, local regulations and zoning laws may impact your ability to rent out rooms within a single-family home. It's crucial to research and understand the legal requirements, permits, and restrictions that apply to shared housing arrangements in your area. Compliance with these regulations ensures a smooth and legally sound operation.

Strategic Investment Considerations: Before embarking on room renting, assess your investment objectives and risk tolerance. Consider factors such as property location, market demand for shared housing, and your capacity for active property management. Properly evaluate potential rental income against costs and risks to determine if this strategy aligns with your overall investment goals.

6. Exploring House Flipping: Transforming Properties for Profit

Understanding House Flipping: House flipping is an investment strategy that entails purchasing distressed or undervalued properties, revitalizing them through strategic renovations, and then selling them swiftly at a higher price point to realize substantial profits. While it offers lucrative potential, it also comes with inherent challenges and requires careful planning.

Navigating the Landscape of Higher Risk and Capital Investment: House flipping stands as a more adventurous avenue within the real estate realm. It demands a higher level of capital investment upfront, encompassing property acquisition costs, renovation expenses, and carrying costs such as mortgage payments and utilities. Additionally, the process may require a significant time commitment before witnessing returns on your investment.

Calculating the After Repair Value (ARV): A pivotal component of successful house flipping is accurately determining the property's After Repair Value (ARV). ARV represents the estimated value of the property after renovations are completed. Calculating ARV involves thorough analysis of comparable properties (comps) in the vicinity that have undergone similar renovations. This approach provides a realistic assessment of the potential resale price and aids in setting a competitive selling price.

Working with Contractors: Balancing Benefits and Challenges: Collaboration with contractors and designers is integral to executing a successful house flipping project. Contractors bring expertise to the table, ensuring renovations are carried out efficiently and up to standard. However, it's essential to strike a balance between the benefits they offer and the challenges that may arise, such as budget overruns, delays, or disagreements on design decisions. Clear communication, detailed project plans, and diligent oversight play a crucial role in managing these dynamics.

Navigating Permits and Code Compliance: As renovations progress and reach a certain threshold, it becomes imperative to secure necessary permits and adhere to modern building codes. Ensuring compliance not only safeguards the integrity of the project but also prevents potential legal and financial liabilities. Working closely with local authorities and building inspectors is essential to navigate this aspect smoothly.

Market Volatility and Timing Considerations: House flipping's profitability is intrinsically tied to market conditions and timing. While renovations are underway, market dynamics can shift, potentially affecting the property's resale value. Fluctuations in local real estate markets emphasize the importance of a solid contingency plan and careful monitoring of market trends throughout the renovation process.

Strategic Renovation Planning and Frustrations: Crafting a detailed renovation plan and budget is paramount for a successful house flipping venture. Thoroughly assess the property's condition and prioritize renovations that maximize value. It's important to anticipate potential challenges, such as unexpected structural issues or design changes, which can lead to frustrations and budget deviations.

Balancing Risk and Reward: House flipping embodies a higher level of risk, making comprehensive research, meticulous planning, and a solid financial cushion imperative. While it requires substantial effort and resources, successful house flipping can yield substantial returns on investment, making it an attractive option for investors willing to navigate its complexities.

Incorporating ARV calculations, managing contractor relationships, navigating permits and code compliance, and accounting for market dynamics are integral components of a well-rounded house flipping strategy. Balancing the potential for profitability with the inherent risks, a successful house flipper combines foresight, strategy, and adaptability to orchestrate a rewarding real estate venture.

Chapter 6:
Commercial Real Estate Investments

Exploring the Commercial Frontier: Diving into Commercial Real Estate Investments

The realm of commercial real estate presents a dynamic landscape of opportunities that extend beyond the boundaries of residential properties. In this chapter, we embark on a journey into the world of commercial real estate investments, where the strategies and considerations differ significantly from those of residential ventures. By unraveling the nuances of property types, lease structures, and risk factors, you will gain a comprehensive understanding of the commercial sector's potential and the tactics required to succeed.

Navigating the Diverse Landscape of Commercial Property Types

Commercial real estate encompasses a wide spectrum of property types, each with distinct characteristics and investment potentials.

Office Spaces: The Hub of Business Activity

Office spaces form the backbone of commercial real estate, serving as the epicenter of business operations. Investing in office properties offers the opportunity to cater to diverse tenants, from startups to established corporations. Understanding location dynamics, tenant preferences, and evolving workspace trends is pivotal in unlocking the potential of office space investments.

Retail Centers: Meeting Consumer Needs

Retail centers, ranging from shopping malls to neighborhood plazas, provide spaces for businesses to connect with consumers. The success of retail investments is closely tied to factors such as foot traffic, tenant mix, and consumer demographics. Investors must grasp the ebb and flow of consumer behavior, technological advancements, and the evolving retail landscape to make informed decisions.

Industrial Properties: Powerhouses of Production

Industrial properties encompass warehouses, distribution centers, and manufacturing facilities that drive commerce and supply chains. Investing in industrial real estate requires an understanding of logistics, transportation networks, and the demands of e-commerce. The rise of online shopping and the need for efficient distribution have reshaped the industrial sector, presenting both challenges and opportunities for investors.

Multifamily Units: Blurring the Line Between Commercial and Residential

Multifamily properties, such as apartment complexes and condominiums, straddle the line between residential and commercial real estate. These investments offer potential for recurring income and diverse tenant pools. Investors must analyze market demand, tenant preferences, and rental trends to optimize the performance of multifamily units in their portfolio.

Deciphering Lease Structures: The Framework of Commercial Transactions

Commercial real estate transactions are underpinned by intricate lease structures that differ significantly from residential arrangements.

Triple Net Leases: Shifting Responsibility to Tenants

Triple net (NNN) leases transfer the burden of property expenses to

Analyzing Office Spaces, Retail Properties, and Industrial Real Estate

In the realm of commercial real estate investments, a strategic analysis of different property types is essential to maximize potential returns and minimize risks. Let's delve into the methodologies and considerations for analyzing office spaces, retail properties, and industrial facilities, each offering unique dynamics and opportunities.

Office Spaces: The Pulse of Business Activity

Analyzing office spaces involves a comprehensive assessment of factors that influence tenant demand, rental income, and long-term value. Consider the following steps:

Location Dynamics: The location of an office space is paramount. Proximity to business districts, transportation hubs, amenities, and urban developments can significantly impact tenant attraction and retention. Research the area's economic health, accessibility, and potential for growth to gauge its suitability for office investments.

Market Demand: Study the demand for office spaces in the chosen location. Identify the target tenant demographic, such as startups, established corporations, or creative enterprises. Analyze vacancy rates, absorption rates, and historical occupancy trends to gauge the level of demand.

Tenant Profiles: Understand the preferences and needs of potential tenants. Are they looking for collaborative open spaces, private offices, or a mix of both? Consider amenities like parking, common areas, and access to public transportation that can enhance tenant satisfaction.

Lease Terms: Evaluate prevailing lease terms in the market, including rental rates, lease lengths, and lease structures. Compare these terms with the property's potential income to ensure favorable cash flow.

Retail Properties: Aligning with Consumer Behavior

Analyzing retail properties requires a deep understanding of consumer behavior, foot traffic, and tenant mix. Here's how to approach the analysis:

Trade Area Analysis: Define the trade area surrounding the retail property, considering factors like population density, income levels, and consumer preferences. Identify the target market and their shopping patterns to ensure the property caters to the right audience.

Tenant Mix: Curate a diverse and complementary tenant mix that caters to different consumer needs. Evaluate tenant creditworthiness, business models, and compatibility with the property's overall theme to reduce vacancy risks and enhance tenant synergy.

Foot Traffic and Visibility: Assess foot traffic data to understand the property's exposure to potential customers. Locations with high foot traffic, visibility from main roads, and proximity to anchor tenants can attract more shoppers and drive tenant success.

E-commerce Compatibility: In the digital age, consider the property's potential for supporting e-commerce initiatives. Retailers may seek spaces that serve as both brick-and-mortar stores and fulfillment centers, bridging the gap between online and offline shopping.

Industrial Facilities: Powering Commerce and Logistics

Analyzing industrial facilities involves evaluating logistical efficiency, supply chain dynamics, and the impact of technological advancements. Here's a framework for analysis:

Logistical Advantage: Examine the facility's proximity to transportation networks, highways, ports, and distribution centers. A strategically located industrial property can streamline supply chain operations and attract tenants seeking efficient transportation.

Technological Infrastructure: Assess the property's readiness for modern technological requirements. Warehouses equipped with advanced automation, inventory tracking systems, and energy-efficient solutions can attract tenants looking to optimize their operations.

E-commerce Potential: Consider the facility's suitability for e-commerce fulfillment and last-mile delivery. The rise of online shopping has driven demand for well-located industrial properties that facilitate rapid order processing and delivery.

Tenant Demand: Analyze the demand for different types of industrial spaces, such as warehouses, distribution centers, or manufacturing facilities. Factors like inventory storage needs, production requirements, and changing consumer behaviors impact tenant demand.

In conclusion, analyzing office spaces, retail properties, and industrial real estate requires a meticulous evaluation of location dynamics, market demand, tenant profiles, lease terms, and other relevant factors. By employing a systematic approach to analysis, you can make informed investment decisions that align with your objectives and capitalize on the unique opportunities presented by each property type.

Lease Structures, Tenant Evaluation, and Property Management

In the realm of commercial real estate investments, lease structures, tenant evaluation, and property management play pivotal roles in determining the success and profitability of your investment. Unlike residential leases, commercial leases are more intricate and tailored to the unique needs of businesses. Let's explore the distinct aspects of commercial leases, tenant evaluation, and property management that are crucial for achieving success in the commercial real estate arena.

Commercial Lease Structures: Tailored to Business Dynamics

Commercial leases diverge significantly from their residential counterparts due to the complexities of business operations. Commercial leases are typically multi-year agreements, often spanning several years, to provide stability for both landlords and tenants. These leases often include built-in, pre-determined price adjustments to account for inflation and market fluctuations over time. Unlike residential leases, which often have fixed monthly rents, commercial leases may include escalation clauses that outline how rent will increase at specified intervals.

Three common types of commercial lease structures are:

Single Net Lease (N Lease): In this lease, the tenant pays base rent and a portion of property taxes, while the landlord covers other expenses like insurance and maintenance.

Double Net Lease (NN Lease): This lease requires the tenant to pay base rent, property taxes, and a share of insurance costs. Maintenance expenses remain the landlord's responsibility.

Triple Net Lease (NNN Lease): In this lease, the tenant covers base rent, property taxes, insurance, and maintenance expenses. This places a significant share of property-related costs on the tenant.

Tenant Evaluation: Navigating Business Histories

When evaluating potential commercial tenants, a deeper assessment is required compared to residential rentals. Consider not only financial stability but also a tenant's business history, skills background, operational knowledge, and track record of successes. Engage in due diligence to verify the authenticity of financial statements, assess business creditworthiness, and understand the potential tenant's ability to uphold lease obligations.

Dig into their business history to understand their experience in the industry, stability, and adaptability to market changes. Evaluate their operational knowledge, as tenants who are well-versed in their field are more likely to maintain a successful enterprise, which in turn benefits the property.

Commercial Property Management: A Different Ballgame

Managing commercial properties involves a distinct set of responsibilities compared to residential properties. The scale of operations and business-oriented nature of commercial real estate necessitate specialized skills and strategies:

Tenant Relationships: Commercial property managers interact with a diverse range of businesses. Establishing and maintaining strong tenant relationships is essential for tenant satisfaction, lease renewals, and attracting new tenants.

Lease Compliance: Ensuring tenants adhere to lease terms, including rent payments and property use, is vital. Property managers also oversee lease renewals, negotiations, and modifications.

Financial Expertise: Commercial property management requires robust financial skills. Property managers handle rent collection, expense tracking, budgeting, and financial reporting for property owners.

Maintenance and Repairs: Property managers coordinate maintenance and repairs to ensure the property meets business needs and regulatory requirements. Prompt response to repair requests and preventive maintenance contribute to tenant satisfaction.

Market Insights: Staying updated on market trends, economic shifts, and local business dynamics informs property management decisions, including lease adjustments and property enhancements.

In summary, commercial lease structures cater to the specific requirements of businesses, featuring multi-year terms and pre-determined adjustments. Evaluating potential commercial tenants involves a comprehensive understanding of their business histories, skills, and operational prowess. Commercial property management encompasses unique responsibilities, including tenant relationships, lease compliance, financial expertise, maintenance, and market insights. By mastering these aspects, you position yourself to navigate the complexities of commercial real estate investments successfully.

Pros and Cons of Commercial Real Estate Investment

Investing in commercial real estate offers a realm of opportunities, each with its own set of advantages and challenges. Understanding the pros and cons of commercial real estate investment is vital to making informed decisions and achieving success in this dynamic and potentially lucrative sector. So let's make a decisional balance sheet or more likely known as a pro's and con's list.

Pros:

Potential for Higher Returns: Commercial properties often yield higher rental income and cash flow compared to residential properties. With businesses as tenants, the income potential is greater, leading to better ROI.

Longer Leases: Commercial leases are typically longer than residential leases, providing more stable cash flow and reduced turnover costs.

Tenant Stability: Businesses tend to remain in one location for longer periods, contributing to greater tenant stability and consistency in income.

Property Appreciation: Well-located commercial properties can appreciate significantly over time, enhancing overall property value.

Diversification: Commercial real estate enables portfolio diversification, reducing risk by spreading investments across various asset types and industries.

Professional Relationships: Commercial real estate often involves forming relationships with professionals such as lawyers, brokers, and property managers, fostering networking and growth opportunities.

Cons:

Higher Initial Investment: Commercial properties typically require a larger upfront investment compared to residential properties, making entry barriers higher.

Tenant Turnover Costs: When tenants change, commercial properties may experience longer periods of vacancy and higher turnover costs.

Market Volatility: Commercial real estate is subject to economic fluctuations and market trends, impacting rental income and property values.

Complexity: Commercial investments involve more complex legal, financial, and operational considerations, requiring a deeper understanding of regulations and market dynamics.

Risk of Economic Downturns: In economic downturns, businesses may struggle, leading to potential rent reductions or vacancies.

Higher Management Demands: Commercial properties often demand more intensive management due to larger spaces, maintenance needs, and lease negotiations.

Specialized Knowledge: Successful commercial real estate investing requires a deeper understanding of market trends, property types, and business dynamics.

Limited Financing Options: Securing financing for commercial properties can be more challenging, and interest rates may be higher than those for residential properties.

Regulatory Compliance: Commercial properties are subject to a range of regulations, including zoning laws, building codes, and accessibility requirements.

Liquidity Concerns: Selling a commercial property can take longer than selling a residential property, potentially affecting access to funds.

In conclusion, commercial real estate investment presents both promising rewards and distinct challenges. While the potential for higher returns, longer leases, and portfolio diversification are enticing, higher initial investment, market volatility, and management demands require careful consideration. Navigating these pros and cons requires a comprehensive understanding of the commercial real estate landscape, an ability to adapt to market shifts, and a strategic approach to building a successful and sustainable portfolio.

Chapter 7:
Scaling Your Real Estate Portfolio

Scaling Your Real Estate Portfolio: From Vision to Reality

In the earlier chapters, we delved deep into the foundational aspects of real estate investing, from crafting a solid investment plan to analyzing properties with precision. As you journeyed through the landscape of real estate, you recognized that flexibility and adaptability are key. Now, armed with your growing expertise and understanding, it's time to take the next bold step: developing a scalable investment strategy.

The Evolution of Your Investment Plan

Remember the investment plan you meticulously crafted back in Chapter 2? That initial blueprint was your compass, guiding you through uncharted waters. But here's the secret: it's not meant to be set in stone. As you gain experience and insights, you'll find yourself revisiting and refining your plan. Your investment journey is an iterative process, where adaptation is your greatest ally.

The Power of Scalability

Scaling your real estate portfolio is a thrilling endeavor that involves expanding your investments and growing your wealth at an accelerated pace. It's about leveraging your successes and learning experiences to venture into new territories while maximizing returns. A well-executed scaling strategy can take your investment journey from a single property to a diversified portfolio, boosting your income potential and financial security.

Paths to Scale Your Real Estate Portfolio

Reinvestment of Income: One of the most effective ways to fuel your scaling efforts is by reinvesting the income generated from your existing properties. Instead of pocketing all your profits, allocate a portion back into your portfolio. This infusion of capital enables you to acquire new properties, diversify your holdings, and amplify your monthly cash flow.

Utilizing OPM (Other People's Money): OPM, or using funds from external sources, can be a game-changer in your scaling journey. By leveraging OPM, you can acquire properties that might have been beyond your initial budget. This can be achieved through partnerships, private lenders, syndications, or crowdfunding platforms. Remember, OPM isn't just about financial capital; it can also mean leveraging other people's time, skills, and expertise.

Exploring Creative Financing: As your portfolio expands, your financial landscape becomes more intricate. Creative financing methods such as seller financing, subject-to deals, or lease options can open doors to properties that align with your scaling strategy. These methods require a deeper understanding of real estate transactions, but they can offer innovative solutions for property acquisition.

Implementing Efficient Systems: Scaling isn't just about acquiring more properties; it's about managing them effectively. Implementing streamlined property management systems and processes ensures that your growing portfolio remains well-maintained and tenant-friendly. Efficient systems also free up your time to focus on strategic decisions and further growth.

Exploring New Markets: Once you've conquered your local market, consider expanding into new geographical areas with strong investment potential. Conduct thorough market research and due diligence to identify emerging markets that align with your investment goals. Diversifying your portfolio across different markets can enhance your risk mitigation and growth opportunities.

The Synergy of Scaling and Strategy

Scaling your real estate portfolio isn't just about acquiring properties haphazardly. It's a delicate dance between growth and strategy. Each step you take should be aligned with your overarching investment plan. As you scale, remember to adapt your plan to accommodate new insights and market dynamics. Your evolving strategy should remain your North Star, guiding you toward long-term success.

Transitioning from Single Properties to a Diverse Portfolio

Your journey through the realm of real estate investing has brought you from the shores of uncertainty to the shores of opportunity. As you stand on the precipice of growth, you may find yourself ready to transition from the world of single properties into the vast expanse of a diverse portfolio. This pivotal step is not just about accumulating more properties; it's about the maturation of your skills and your evolution as a seasoned investor.

The Maturity of Skills: From Novice to Savvy Investor

Think back to when you first embarked on your real estate journey. You might have started with a single-family home, navigating the intricate process of property acquisition, financing, and management. Each step was a learning experience, building the foundation of your expertise.

With every property you acquired, your skills matured. You honed your ability to identify profitable deals, negotiate favorable terms, and navigate complex transactions. You gained a deeper understanding of market trends, property valuation, and risk mitigation. This growth in knowledge and skill positions you to take on more complex and diverse investments.

Diversification: Redefining Risk and Reward

Transitioning to a diverse portfolio is not just about quantity; it's about redefining your risk and reward equation. While single properties have their merits, a diverse portfolio offers a level of stability and income potential that transcends the confines of a single investment.

Diversification spreads risk across various property types, markets, and asset classes. It cushions your portfolio against downturns in specific sectors and provides a more balanced income stream. Your evolving expertise allows you to identify opportunities in different markets, from multifamily homes to commercial properties, and even large-scale residential buildings.

Unlocking Commercial Real Estate: The Next Frontier

As you ascend the ladder of real estate success, the allure of commercial real estate beckons. Commercial properties offer a new dimension of investment potential, characterized by larger scales, diversified income streams, and unique value propositions.

Transitioning into commercial real estate requires a refined skill set and an understanding of the intricacies that differentiate it from residential properties. From office spaces and retail properties to industrial complexes, each sector presents distinct challenges and opportunities. Evaluating lease structures, analyzing tenant profiles, and conducting thorough due diligence become essential components of your investment strategy.

Charting Your Course: From Growth to Legacy

Your transition from single properties to a diverse portfolio is a testament to your growth and resilience as an investor. It signifies your ability to adapt, learn, and capitalize on the ever-changing landscape of real estate. As you venture into commercial real estate and large-scale residential buildings, you're not just building a portfolio; you're crafting a legacy.

Your evolving skills, supported by the lessons learned from each property, guide you toward new horizons. With every investment decision, you're shaping your financial future and leaving a mark on the world of real estate. The journey from novice to savvy investor is a path of transformation, and your ability to embrace change is the compass that leads you toward greater success.

Building Your Winning Team: Unveiling the Power of Professionals

One of the most crucial elements of your success lies in the assembly of your winning team. Just as a conductor relies on a symphony of instruments to create a harmonious melody, you, as an investor, need a skilled ensemble of professionals to orchestrate your real estate endeavors. This team, consisting of real estate agents, lawyers, accountants, and property managers, is the backbone of your operation, propelling you toward your investment goals with precision and expertise.

The Maestro of Market Insight: Your Real Estate Agent

A knowledgeable and experienced real estate agent is your trusted guide through the labyrinthine corridors of property acquisition and disposition. They possess an intimate understanding of local markets, enabling them to identify promising properties aligned with your investment strategy. From scouting potential deals to negotiating terms, your agent is your advocate, ensuring you make informed decisions and secure optimal deals.

The Legal Luminary: Your Real Estate Lawyer

The legal landscape of real estate transactions can be treacherous to navigate alone. That's where your real estate lawyer steps in, armed with a wealth of legal acumen. They meticulously review contracts, ensuring compliance with local regulations and safeguarding your interests. Their expertise helps you traverse the legal complexities, from due diligence to title searches, ensuring a seamless and secure transaction.

The Financial Virtuoso: Your Accountant

In the intricate world of real estate, the financial puzzle must be meticulously assembled. Enter your accountant, armed with insights into tax strategies and financial planning. They help you optimize ownership structures, maximize returns, and minimize tax liabilities. With their guidance, you navigate the fiscal intricacies of your investments, ensuring your wealth-building journey remains on a solid financial foundation.

The Property Maestro: Your Property Manager

Scaling your portfolio often means managing a multitude of properties, each requiring attention, maintenance, and tenant relations. Here, your property manager steps into the spotlight. They oversee day-to-day operations, handling tenant inquiries, maintenance requests, and ensuring your investments run like a well-oiled machine. Their efficient management frees your time and focus, allowing you to continue growing your portfolio.

The Synchronized Symphony of Your Team

While each professional brings a unique skill set to the table, the true power of your team lies in their harmonious collaboration. Their synergy amplifies the impact of your investments, allowing you to navigate challenges and capitalize on opportunities with confidence. Together, they help you execute your investment plan, adapting to the evolving landscape and keeping your portfolio aligned with your strategy.

The Essential Alignment: Fitting into Your Strategy

It's important to note that your team doesn't have to be flawless; they need to be aligned with your strategy and possess an understanding of your investment plan. Just as a well-rehearsed orchestra produces a captivating performance, your team's knowledge of your strategy enhances their ability to work together seamlessly. They share a common goal: your success.

In your journey of scaling your real estate portfolio, remember that building your team is an investment in itself. The professionals you select become an integral part of your narrative, supporting you as you venture into new territories and strive for greater heights. With your team in place, you're poised to embark on a journey where every note of success is a testament to the collaborative masterpiece you've created.

Chapter 8:
Realizing Returns: Exit Strategies

Selling Properties for Profit:

The decision to sell a property is a pivotal moment in your real estate journey. While market conditions play a role, the art of timing the market is more intricate than it seems. Rather than attempting to predict market highs and lows, focus on aligning your sale with your personal objectives and future plans.

The Challenge of Timing the Market

Timing the market can be an elusive pursuit. Market fluctuations are influenced by a myriad of factors beyond an investor's control, making accurate predictions difficult. Attempting to sell at the market's peak often leads to missed opportunities or substantial holding costs.

Making Selling a Personal Decision

Rather than chasing elusive market timing, consider selling properties based on your unique circumstances. Are you aiming to cash out for a new investment? Is the property no longer aligned with your goals? Personal motivations, such as retiring, relocating, or diversifying your portfolio, should guide your decision.

1031 Exchanges and Tax Implications: The Art of Deferred Gain

A 1031 exchange is a powerful tool in an investor's arsenal, allowing you to defer capital gains taxes while transitioning from one investment to another. This strategic maneuver opens opportunities for portfolio growth and asset enhancement.

Understanding the 1031 Exchange

A 1031 exchange, also known as a like-kind exchange, permits you to sell a property and reinvest the proceeds into another similar property without recognizing capital gains. This enables you to maintain equity and leverage while upgrading or diversifying your portfolio.

Benefits of a 1031 Exchange

The primary advantage of a 1031 exchange is the tax deferral, which preserves more of your funds for reinvestment. This process facilitates portfolio growth and provides flexibility in adapting to changing market conditions. By deferring taxes, you have more capital to invest, potentially accelerating your wealth-building journey.

Challenges and Considerations

While 1031 exchanges offer significant benefits, they are subject to strict rules and timelines. Identifying a replacement property within 45 days and completing the exchange within 180 days requires careful planning and execution. Additionally, depreciation recapture taxes may still apply, and choosing properties that truly align with your goals is paramount.

Legacy Planning: Passing on Real Estate Assets to Heirs

As your real estate journey unfolds, a crucial consideration is how to pass on your hard-earned assets to future generations. Thoughtful legacy planning ensures that your investments continue to benefit your heirs and align with their aspirations.

Exploring Trusts and Future Generations

One strategy for mitigating heir taxes and preserving your legacy is establishing a trust. Trusts provide a structured mechanism to pass on real estate assets while offering control over how the assets are managed and distributed. This approach ensures your properties continue to contribute to your family's prosperity for generations to come.

Consulting Your Tax Professional

While legacy planning holds great potential, it's essential to collaborate with a qualified tax professional who understands your unique circumstances. Your tax advisor can tailor strategies to your financial goals and family dynamics, ensuring that your legacy endures with maximum benefit and minimal tax impact.

Chapter 9:
The Path to Financial Freedom

As your real estate journey unfolds, you'll witness a remarkable phenomenon at play – the compounding of value and the gradual accumulation of wealth. This chapter delves into how the synergy of appreciation, mortgage payments, and strategic investing can transform your properties into a potent wealth-building engine. Along the way, you'll discover how real estate can provide not only long-term financial security but also a semi-passive income stream to fuel your aspirations.

The Power of Compounding Value

Real estate's unique ability to appreciate over time is the cornerstone of your wealth-building engine. As properties appreciate, their value compounds, multiplying your initial investment. Historical data underscores the potential for substantial long-term gains, as properties in well-chosen markets have exhibited consistent appreciation, outpacing inflation and other investment vehicles.

The Mortgage Paydown Effect

Each mortgage payment you make contributes to the gradual reduction of your property's debt. This dual process – the increase in property value and the reduction of debt – fuels a compounding effect that progressively enhances your equity position. Over time, your ownership stake in the property grows, providing you with a powerful wealth-building mechanism.

Creating Semi-Passive Income

While real estate requires ongoing management and oversight, the strategic utilization of property management services and efficient systems can transform your investment into a semi-passive income stream. By outsourcing day-to-day tasks such as tenant management, maintenance, and rent collection, you free up your time while preserving the income flow from your properties.

Building a Future of Wealth

The culmination of compounding value, mortgage paydown, and semi-passive income sets the stage for a future brimming with wealth and financial security. As your portfolio matures, your equity position strengthens, allowing you to make strategic decisions based on your evolving goals – whether that involves expanding your portfolio, diversifying into new markets, or enjoying the fruits of your labor.

Chapter 10:
Conclusion - Your Journey to Real Estate Success

Congratulations! You've embarked on an exciting and transformative journey into the world of real estate investing. As you reach the conclusion of this book, take a moment to reflect on the progress you've made and the invaluable knowledge you've acquired. You've learned the fundamentals, strategies, and tools needed to navigate the dynamic landscape of real estate and build a thriving portfolio.

Reflecting on Your Progress

Remember when you first started this journey? You delved into the intricacies of real estate, from understanding market cycles and property analysis to financing options and building a skilled team. With each step, you gained insights that empowered you to make informed decisions and seize opportunities. Take pride in how far you've come, from a beginner investor to someone equipped with the tools to navigate the complexities of real estate.

A Positive Outlook on Investing

Real estate investing is a journey of growth, empowerment, and financial freedom. The world of real estate offers boundless opportunities for those who are willing to learn, adapt, and take action. While challenges and uncertainties may arise, your newfound knowledge and skills will enable you to navigate them with confidence. Embrace a positive outlook on investing, knowing that your dedication and perseverance will lead you to success.

Continuing Your Learning Journey

As you close this chapter, remember that your journey is far from over. The world of real estate is ever-evolving, and there's always more to learn, explore, and achieve. Continue expanding your knowledge through books, courses, seminars, and networking opportunities. Surround yourself with like-minded individuals who share your passion for real estate and are eager to exchange insights and experiences.

Encouragement to Keep Growing

Building a real estate portfolio and accumulating wealth is a process that unfolds over time. Patience and persistence are key virtues as you nurture your investments and watch them flourish. Embrace the lessons you've learned, both from successes and challenges, as they contribute to your growth as an investor. Your journey is uniquely yours, and every step you take brings you closer to your financial goals.

Your Future Awaits

As you conclude this book, remember that the path you've embarked upon holds immense potential. The journey to real estate success is not just about accumulating properties; it's about creating a legacy, securing your financial future, and realizing your dreams. With your newfound knowledge and determination, you have the power to shape your destiny and build a real estate portfolio that stands as a testament to your hard work and vision.

So, take a deep breath, stand tall, and step forward with confidence. Your journey in real estate has only just begun, and the future is brimming with possibilities. Continue growing your real estate portfolio, building wealth, and embracing the remarkable journey that lies ahead. Your success story in real estate is waiting to be written – go out there and make it happen!

Appendices:

Glossary of key real estate investment terms

ROI (Return on Investment): Definition: ROI is a financial metric used to evaluate the profitability of an investment. It measures the ratio of net profit to the initial investment. Equation: ROI = (Net Profit / Initial Investment) x 100

NOI (Net Operating Income): Definition: NOI is the total revenue generated from a property after subtracting operating expenses but before deducting interest and taxes. It's a key indicator of the property's cash flow potential. Equation: NOI = Gross Income - Operating Expenses

Cap Rate (Capitalization Rate): Definition: Cap rate is a percentage representing the relationship between the property's net operating income and its market value. It helps investors assess the potential return on their investment. Equation: Cap Rate = (NOI / Property Value) x 100

Cash Flow: Definition: Cash flow is the net amount of money generated from an investment property after deducting all expenses from rental income. Equation: Cash Flow = Rental Income - Operating Expenses

Gross Rent Multiplier (GRM): Definition: GRM is a quick way to estimate the value of an income-producing property based on its gross rental income. It's often used for preliminary property evaluations. Equation: GRM = Property Price / Gross Rental Income

Debt Service Coverage Ratio (DSCR): Definition: DSCR is a measure of a property's ability to cover its debt obligations from its net operating income. Lenders often use this ratio to assess loan eligibility. Equation: DSCR = NOI / Annual Debt Service

Cash-on-Cash Return: Definition: Cash-on-cash return calculates the annual income generated from an investment property in relation to the initial cash invested. Equation: Cash-on-Cash Return = (Annual Cash Flow / Initial Investment) x 100

Break-Even Ratio: Definition: The break-even ratio determines the occupancy rate needed to cover operating expenses and mortgage payments. Equation: Break-Even Ratio = Operating Expenses / Effective Gross Income

Loan-to-Value Ratio (LTV): Definition: LTV is the ratio of the loan amount to the property's appraised value. It's used to assess the riskiness of a mortgage loan. Equation: LTV = (Loan Amount / Property Value) x 100

Internal Rate of Return (IRR): Definition: IRR represents the average annual rate of return an investor can expect to receive over the life of an investment, accounting for the timing and magnitude of cash flows. Equation: Solve for the discount rate that makes the Net Present Value (NPV) of all cash flows equal to zero.

DTI (Debt-to-Income Ratio): Definition: DTI is a ratio that measures a borrower's monthly debt payments relative to their gross monthly income. Lenders use DTI to assess a borrower's ability to manage additional debt.

Credit Score: Definition: A credit score is a numerical representation of a person's creditworthiness. It is based on their credit history, outstanding debts, payment history, and other financial factors.

LTV (Loan-to-Value Ratio): Definition: LTV is the ratio of the loan amount to the appraised value or purchase price of the property. It helps lenders evaluate the risk associated with a mortgage loan.

APR (Annual Percentage Rate): Definition: APR is the total cost of borrowing, including interest and fees, expressed as an annual percentage of the loan amount. It allows borrowers to compare the true cost of different loan options.

PMI (Private Mortgage Insurance): Definition: PMI is a type of insurance that lenders may require borrowers to purchase if their down payment is less than 20% of the home's value. It protects the lender in case of default.

ARM (Adjustable Rate Mortgage): Definition: An ARM is a mortgage with an interest rate that adjusts periodically based on a specified index. Initial rates are typically lower than fixed-rate mortgages but can increase over time.

FICO Score: Definition: A FICO score is a credit score calculated using the FICO scoring model. It is widely used by lenders to assess credit risk and determine interest rates for loans.

PITI (Principal, Interest, Taxes, Insurance): Definition: PITI represents the four components of a monthly mortgage payment. It includes the principal and interest payments, property taxes, and homeowner's insurance.

GFE (Good Faith Estimate): Definition: A GFE is a document provided by lenders to borrowers that outlines the estimated costs associated with obtaining a mortgage loan, including closing costs.

Escrow: Definition: Escrow is a third-party account where funds are held and managed during a real estate transaction. It ensures that money is securely held until all terms and conditions are met.

Closing Costs: Definition: Closing costs are fees and expenses associated with finalizing a real estate transaction. They include fees for appraisal, title search, attorney services, and more.

Interest Rate: Definition: The interest rate is the cost of borrowing money, expressed as a percentage. It determines the amount of interest the borrower will pay over the life of the loan.

Prequalification: Definition: Prequalification is an initial assessment of a borrower's creditworthiness and ability to qualify for a mortgage. It is not a guarantee of loan approval.

Preapproval: Definition: Preapproval is a more comprehensive process where a lender evaluates a borrower's credit, income, and financial documentation to determine the maximum loan amount they are eligible for

Driving for Dollars: Definition: Driving for dollars involves physically driving through neighborhoods to identify distressed or vacant properties. Investors look for signs of neglect, such as overgrown lawns or boarded-up windows, as potential opportunities for investment.

Door Knocking: Definition: Door knocking is a proactive approach where investors visit property owners in person, often to discuss potential selling opportunities. This method allows for direct communication and building personal connections.

Mailing Campaigns: Definition: Mailing campaigns involve sending targeted direct mail to property owners, such as postcards or letters. These materials may express interest in purchasing their property or offering solutions for distressed situations.

Cold Calling: Definition: Cold calling is the practice of reaching out to property owners by phone, often without prior contact, to discuss potential real estate deals. This method requires effective communication skills and a script.

Wholesaling: Definition: Wholesaling involves finding distressed properties, getting them under contract at a discounted price, and then assigning the contract to another investor for a fee. Wholesalers facilitate the transaction without taking ownership of the property.

Networking: Definition: Networking involves building relationships within the real estate industry, including fellow investors, real estate agents, brokers, and professionals. Networking events, online platforms, and real estate clubs can provide valuable connections.

Online Marketing: Definition: Online marketing includes using websites, social media, and online advertisements to attract potential sellers or buyers. This method leverages digital platforms to reach a wider audience.

Real Estate Agents: Definition: Real estate agents are licensed professionals who assist buyers and sellers in real estate transactions. They can help investors find properties, negotiate deals, and provide market insights.

Auctions: Definition: Real estate auctions involve competitive bidding on properties, often resulting in properties being sold quickly and at potentially favorable prices. Auctions can be conducted online or in-person.

MLS (Multiple Listing Service): Definition: The MLS is a database used by real estate agents to list properties for sale. Investors can access the MLS through an agent or brokerage to search for potential investment opportunities.

HUD Homes: Definition: HUD (U.S. Department of Housing and Urban Development) homes are properties owned by the government due to foreclosure on FHA-insured mortgages. These properties are often sold at discounted prices.

Probate Properties: Definition: Probate properties are properties owned by individuals who have passed away, and their estates are going through the probate process. These properties may be sold by heirs or executors of the estate.

Real Estate Wholesalers: Definition: Wholesalers are individuals or companies that specialize in finding distressed properties and then selling them to investors at a marked-up price. They play a role in connecting buyers and sellers.

Networking with Attorneys and Probate Specialists: Definition: Building relationships with attorneys and probate specialists can provide access to off-market deals, particularly properties going through probate or legal proceedings.

Fix and Flip: Definition: The fix and flip strategy involves purchasing a distressed property, renovating or improving it, and then quickly selling it for a profit. Investors aim to enhance the property's value through renovations to attract higher offers from buyers.

Buy and Hold: Definition: The buy and hold strategy involves acquiring a property with the intention of holding it as a long-term investment. Investors generate rental income from tenants while benefiting from potential property appreciation over time.

Wholesaling: Definition: Wholesaling can also be an exit strategy for selling real estate. Wholesalers assign a contract for a property to another investor, typically for a fee. They do not take ownership of the property but facilitate the transaction.

Seller Financing: Definition: Seller financing, also known as owner financing, involves the property owner acting as the lender for the buyer. The buyer makes regular payments directly to the seller, often with interest, instead of obtaining a traditional mortgage.

Lease Option or Rent-to-Own: Definition: In a lease option or rent-to-own arrangement, the buyer leases the property with the option to purchase it at a predetermined price within a specified period. This strategy provides flexibility for potential buyers who may not qualify for traditional financing immediately.

1031 Exchange: Definition: A 1031 exchange is a tax-deferred strategy where an investor sells a property and uses the proceeds to acquire another like-kind property. By doing so, the investor can defer capital gains taxes on the sale.

Cash Purchase: Definition: A cash purchase involves buying a property with cash, eliminating the need for mortgage financing. This strategy can provide a competitive advantage in negotiations and streamline the purchasing process.

Auction Sale: Definition: Auction sales involve selling a property through a competitive bidding process. Properties are typically sold to the highest bidder, often resulting in a quicker sale. Auctions can be conducted online or in-person.

Leaseback: Definition: In a leaseback arrangement, the property seller becomes a tenant by leasing the property back from the buyer. This can be a useful strategy for sellers who want to access the equity in their property while continuing to occupy it.

Private Sale: Definition: A private sale involves selling a property directly to a buyer without listing it on the open market. This strategy may allow for more personalized negotiations and potentially a quicker sale.

Seller Buydown: Definition: A seller buydown involves the property seller paying a portion of the buyer's mortgage interest for a specified period. This can make the property more attractive to buyers by reducing their initial mortgage payments.

Partial Ownership Sale: Definition: In a partial ownership sale, the property owner sells a percentage of ownership to another party. This strategy can provide liquidity to the seller while allowing them to retain partial ownership and potential future profits.

Reverse Mortgage: Definition: A reverse mortgage allows homeowners, typically seniors, to convert part of their home equity into cash. The homeowner receives regular payments from a lender based on the property's value.

Resources for further education and market research

BiggerPockets: A comprehensive online platform offering articles, forums, podcasts, and educational content for real estate investors of all experience levels.

Investopedia - Real Estate Section: A valuable resource providing in-depth articles, tutorials, and guides on various aspects of real estate investing and finance.

The Motley Fool - Real Estate Investing Section: Offers insights and advice on real estate investing, including articles on property analysis, financing, and market trends.

Real Estate Investment Association (REIA) Groups: Local REIA groups provide networking opportunities, educational events, and access to experienced investors within your region.

YouTube Channels: Channels like Graham Stephan, Meet Kevin, and BiggerPockets offer video content covering real estate investing strategies, tips, and case studies.

Books on Real Estate Investing: Books by authors like Robert Kiyosaki ("Rich Dad Poor Dad"), Brandon Turner ("The Book on Rental Property Investing"), and J. Scott ("The Book on Flipping Houses") provide in-depth insights into different investment strategies.

Podcasts: Podcasts such as "The Real Estate Guys Radio Show," "The Real Estate Rookie Podcast," and "Passive Real Estate Investing" deliver informative discussions with industry experts.

Local Real Estate Agents: Experienced local real estate agents can provide insights into market trends, property values, and investment opportunities in your area.

Real Estate Blogs: Numerous blogs, such as Mashvisor, Afford Anything, and Coach Carson, share real-world experiences, strategies, and advice for investors.

Real Estate Investment Conferences: Attending real estate investment conferences and seminars, such as the National Real Estate Investors Association (NREIA) events, can offer valuable educational sessions and networking opportunities.

Sample investment plan and property analysis worksheets

Property Analysis Worksheet:

_Property Details__:_

Property Address: _____

Property Type: _____

Purchase Price: $_____

Estimated Renovation Costs: $_____

Total Investment: $_____

Income:

Monthly Rent: $_____

Annual Rent: $_____

Other Income (e.g., storage, parking): $_____

Total Annual Income: $_____

Expenses:

Property Taxes: $_____

Insurance: $_____

Property Management: $_____

Repairs/Maintenance: $_____

Vacancy (estimated percentage): _____%

Other Expenses: $_____

Total Annual Expenses: $_____

Cash Flow:

Gross Operating Income (GOI): $_____ (Annual Rent + Other Income)

Net Operating Income (NOI): $_____ (GOI - Total Expenses)

Monthly Cash Flow: $_____ (NOI / 12)

Return on Investment (ROI):

Cash on Cash ROI: _____% (Annual Cash Flow / Total Investment)

Cap Rate: _____% (NOI / Purchase Price)

Financing:

Down Payment: $_____

Loan Amount: $_____ (Total Investment - Down Payment)

Loan Interest Rate: _____%

Loan Term: _____ years

Monthly Loan Payment: $_____

Total Cash Invested:

Down Payment: $_____

Renovation Costs: $_____

Other Initial Costs: $_____

Total Cash Invested: $_____

Potential ROI Scenarios:

Best Case Scenario: _____% (Higher Rent, Lower Expenses)

Worst Case Scenario: _____% (Lower Rent, Higher Expenses)